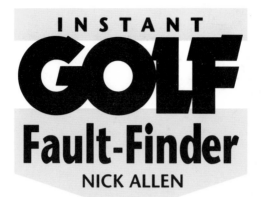

INSTANT GOLF Fault-Finder

NICK ALLEN

FAULT FINDERS

First published in 1992 by
Ashford, Buchan & Enright
31 Bridge Street, Leatherhead, Surrey

British Library Cataloguing in Publication Data

Allen Nick
Instant Golf Fault Finder
I. Title
796.352

ISBN 1-85253-270-X

Designed and produced by
SP Creative Design
Linden House, Kings Road, Bury St Edmunds, Suffolk
Art Director: Rolando Ugolini
Editor: Heather Thomas
Photographs: Rolando Ugolini

The publishers would like to thank Greg Dukart,
Head Professional at East Sussex National Golf Club
for his help and allowing us to take photographs
at the course.

Typeset by Halcyon Type & Design, Ipswich, Suffolk
Origination by Graphicolour, Thurston, Suffolk
Printed and bound in Great Britain by The Bath Press,
Bath, Avon.

Contents

The author

Nick Allen is a PGA Professional and consultant with Apollo Golf Shafts, which operates a Tour Support Service on the European Tour. He has played extensively on the professional circuit both in the United States and Europe. He is also the director of a golf course development company. Nick Allen lives in Kent, England.

CHAPTER ONE

The set up

Standing too close

Standing the correct distance from the ball will allow you to form the correct posture, in particular the angle of the trunk which will influence your turning motion and swing plane.

1 Frequently golfers stand too close to the ball forming an upright posture where the centre of gravity is too high (right) in the legs, not anchoring the player at address.

2 During the set up, try and raise your toes; if you can do this, you have too much weight on your heels (below). You should extend the club further away until you feel the weight more on the balls of your feet.

3 If you are standing the correct distance from the ball and forming a sound posture, you should feel the centre of gravity pulled towards the ankles and through to the balls of the feet.

4 It is important to have the lie of your clubs checked. If the lie is too upright for you, the tendency is to stand too far from the ball. The effect of this is to raise the toe of the club off the ground, which will close the club face at impact.

Distance and posture exercise

1 Stand upright with knees slightly flexed.
2 Bend forwards carefully from the waist while retaining the knee flex.

Positioning the ball

The factors that will affect the ball strike and subsequent flight are: swing speed, plane, path, angle of attack and the position of the ball. Golfers of all standards frequently make mistakes with ball placement.

1 If the ball is positioned too far back in the stance, the angle between the left arm and club shaft cannot recover in time, and turf contact and a skyed flight that lacks power often result as the hands lead and the club head descends steeply.

2 If the ball is too far back in relation to the intended position when using an iron, the steep angle of attack can promote a push or a fat shot.

3 Using a simple pre-shot routine will encourage correct ball positioning. Approach the ball by taking a small step forwards with your right foot at angles to the target line and slightly behind the ball while simultaneously grounding the club. Retain this position for a few moments, then position the right foot further behind the ball and move the left foot slightly wide of the ball. The right foot will move wider to establish its forward position.

Establish a central ball position

Place the right foot at right angles to the target line and slightly behind the ball (above). Position the left foot behind the line of the right foot, then slide to meet the line (above right). The right foot moves wider (right).

Practice routine
for woods

1 To establish the correct driver/ball position, place the right foot slightly further behind the ball.
2 Slide the left foot slightly beyond the ball.
3 Slide the right foot wider than you do with an iron to establish a forward ball position.

Short irons

A short iron shot requires a steeper downswing plane than does the driver. The angle between the left arm and the club shaft is retained longer during the downswing where the ball position facilitates the descending club head angle of attack.

The flatter plane

The flatter plane to the driver swing produces a shallow angle of attack (below). As the club head reaches the bottom of its arc, it passes momentarily horizontal with the ground (right) and sweeps the ball from its position just inside the left heel.

Visualization

This is the key to checking the ball position. As you look down from the playing position, imagine a line from the back of the ball that intersects at right angles a line across your toes. Use the twin club drill shown (right) to check your ball position during practice.

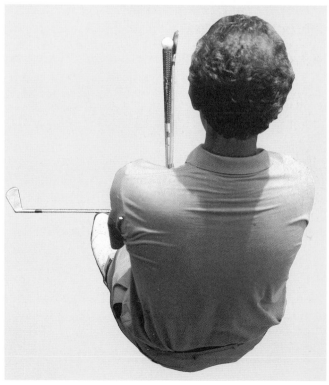

Correct ball positions for irons

This photograph shows the correct ball positions for different irons:
A *is the position for short irons;*
B *for middle irons; and* **C** *for long irons.*

Grip pressure

Your hands transmit the 'feel' of the club through to your senses, so a sound grip and the correct amount of pressure are necessary to allow the swing to function.

1 An instinctive habit with many golfers encourages tension in the grip by continually regripping and moving the fingers (right)

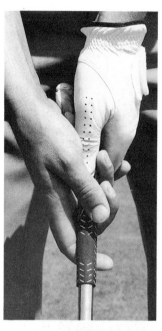

even after the set up has been taken. This leads to a sudden tightening of the hands as the swing begins, often locking the wrist set process in the backswing. Similarly, grip pressure that is too loose (below) in the set up will tighten instinctively during the takeaway with similar consequences.

2 If the grip of the club is not positioned correctly within the left hand, the grip may slip during the backswing (left) causing a change of club face angle. The sudden tightening can produce a flailing action, steepening the angle of attack.

3 Establish your grip before committing your set up (below). Squeeze the grip pressure points shown and try and maintain this pressure without regripping and moving the fingers. Remember that there is always an instinctive tightening of the grip as the club starts away.

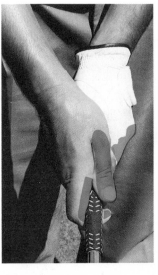

With the grip positioned incorrectly in the left hand (top), the club will overswing and the left arm collapse (left). The pressure points are shown (above).

CHAPTER TWO

The swing

Wrists cocking too early in the backswing

The timing of the wrist set on the backswing will influence the downswing angle of attack and subsequent contact with the ball.

1 The strong grip is a frequent problem; if it is excessive to the extent that the wrists have turned to face the direction of the backswing, an early, and sometimes immediate, set will occur (right). The angle between the left arm and club shaft will be so acute that it cannot recover effectively on the downswing (below), usually resulting in a fat iron shot, or a steep

(divot) skyed drive. To loosen grip pressure as the swing starts can encourage early set.

2 If the right hand is gripping too tightly, it can snatch the club away influencing an early wrist break. Refer to the pressure pointers on page 18, and feel the left hand initiate the takeaway. As the hands approach hip height, the wrists begin to set.

3 The turn and motion of the swing unit continues as the wrists set gradually. The emphasis is on a 'feeling' of the setting action blending in with the swing motion. Refer to the photographic sequence shown here.

Tension at address

Tension at address affects the timing of the swing action and will certainly lead to mishit shots. A number of factors create this problem, although by focusing on certain routines tension can be eradicated.

1 Excessive tension in the grip can spread into the arms and shoulders effectively locking the swing unit at address. There are two well documented 'tips' that golfers frequently offer as advice to one another: "Keep

your left arm straight" and "Keep your head down". However, these points are often taken to excess and may even encourage tension.

The swing unit is hanging in the natural position (opposite). A tight grip (right) will spread muscular tension, causing the left elbow to lock, forcing the left shoulder upwards. If you exaggerate the frequently given advice of keeping the head down and the left arm straight (below), you force the body to straighten and thereby restrict free extension and club head speed.

2 Standing too far from the ball can also encourage tension. Without a club, assume your posture with your hands held at your side (above). If your posture is correct, 'freeing' your arms will let them hang naturally (above left). See how they extend further with the weight of the club pulling them into position at address (right).

3 Review your distance with the drill shown on page 8. Observe the routine of other players at address; it is vital that you waggle the club and acknowledge the target a couple of times. In addition, light foot movement will break tension prior to starting the swing.

Swing path on the backswing

A sound address position promotes a good start to the swing, but it is still important to understand the concept of swing path and its correlation with the body turn.

Immediately the swing begins, the left side (knee, hip, shoulder) responds in

At address, focus on starting the swing unit in unison (inset left). As the hands approach hip height (below), the wrists begin to set.

unison. The club head travels on the target line until the turning motion influences the path to move inside the line as the swing progresses to the top where the club shaft is parallel with the target line.

The view from above shows that by allowing the club face position to alter gradually and in unison with the turn (top), the back of the left hand and club face point outwards as the club reaches waist height. A sound start to the swing positions the club shaft parallel with the target line at the top (above). This is the perfect position from which to start the downswing.

Club face position and control

Beginners and even more established players often fall into a trap regarding club face position and control.

1 During the takeaway the hands should not consciously influence the position of the club face (inset). A common fault is either a roll open, or a resistance to close the face (below).

2 From a good grip and set up, if the motion of the hands and arms (swing unit) commence simultaneously with the turn, and no tension is present, the club face position will alter in time with the turn, not through a conscious move.

Club face
control exercise

1 Set up carefully and initiate the takeaway (slow simulation).

2 Stop at any point and ground the club.

3 Turn your body clockwise and adjust your set up naturally. The club face position should be perfectly square to an imaginary target line. Do this a few times, stopping and checking at different points. The check will identify a closed or open blade during the takeaway. This exercise will increase your perception of club face control. Looking into a mirror, observe the club face position during your backswing, and frequently check the face position at the top of the swing.

Loss of control from the top of the backswing

This problem is commonly referred to as casting the club from the top of the swing. It creates general inconsistency, i.e. topped and fatted shots, and it is also a major power leak in the golf swing.

As the swing unit approaches hip height, the wrist set should have commenced (above) but tension and an excessively tight grip have nullified this process. This causes the left arm to collapse and distribute too much weight onto the left leg (top right). In an effort to create width in the downswing, the hands have thrown the club head from the top (above), forcing the weight onto the right leg.

1 Tension at address can nullify the timing of the wrist set. Similarly, a strong grip can delay the process to the extent that when the wrists do break late in the swing, the left arm collapses causing an instinctive 'cast' to create some width in the downswing.

2 A loose grip (right) can also affect this timing. As the swing starts a sudden increase in pressure locks the swing unit. If the club is not held correctly in either hand, particularly the left, it may loosen at the top of the backswing, and the instinctive tightening will again cause a 'snatch'.

A common problem is simply a misunderstanding of the unity required between the swing unit and the left side of the body, often causing a tilt and lateral hip move.

3 Check your distance away from the ball. Posture has an effect on your ability to retain a good width of arc.

If the pressure is too loose prior to the start (opposite), it will be too tight as the swing begins, and this can delay the wrist set. Positioning the grip incorrectly in the left hand

(above) causes the fingers to open as the backswing is completed.

The perfect club face position at the top of the backswing (above). Practise this at home in front of a mirror where you can turn and check your position.

Practice drill

Place a target line reference on the ground and assume your set up. Practise timing the start, i.e. swing unit and left side unity. 'Feel' the timing of the wrist set, in particular the 'blend'. Once the angle is set, it remains in that position to the top of the backswing. Allow yourself to complete the turn and emphasise the pull (leverage) from the left hand to start the downswing.

The key is to feel the wrist set gradually and allow this process to blend in with the motion of the body turn and arm swing. This sequence of photos to the top of the backswing demonstrates this.

At the start of the downswing, the left hand pulls, creating the leverage that controls the timing of the club head delivery.

The shoulders usually turn on a plane set by the angle of the spine at address (opposite). This can also be influenced by sliding the hips laterally, and lifting the arms to start the swing, which can create this steep-angled tilt of the shoulders.

Poor shoulder turn

A full shoulder turn will maximize the length of your arc which will have a direct effect on distance; it will also help to position the club ready for the downswing. Furthermore, it allows time for the correct sequence of movement.

1 A common fault is the tilt often caused by standing too close to the ball. It can also be caused by an early wrist set or lateral slide of the hips. Reaching for the ball will influence a flat swing path, and the shoulders will turn on a flat plane. The correct posture will turn the shoulders on a plane midway between the two, around the axis formed by the posture at address.

An upright trunk position at address (top) or a takeaway that moves inside the line too early can produce a flat swing plane and shoulder turn. The correct posture and start to the swing (above) allows the shoulders to turn on the correct plane.

2 Another common fault is starting the hands and arms independently of the body. This results in an incomplete shoulder turn. The club gets 'laid off', encouraging a spin out of the shoulders on the downswing.

When the turn is incomplete at the top (below), the hands and arms start to swing first, outpacing the turn. When the body turn is restricted (right), and the hands and arms move independently, the incomplete shoulder turn lays the club off to the left of the target.

3 First ensure that you are aiming correctly – check this with the twin club drill on page 15. Correct alignment will allow you to sense a full turn.

Practice drill

If possible stand in front of a mirror, check your distance from the ball and feel during the takeaway that you are initiating the pivotal turn immediately the swing begins. During this move, feel that you are turning around an imaginary axis through the body; the turn and swing unit should function at the same speed.

Stick an old shaft in the ground or lay a club midway between your feet as an axis around which to turn (above). Focus on feeling the left arm start the swing and allow 1, 2 and 3 to respond in unison.

Feeling the turn build around a central axis will position a greater proportion of weight into the right side – the desired position (above). If your flexibility allows you to swing to horizontal in a controlled position with a good width of arc, this is acceptable.

Backswing too short or too long

Your first consideration regarding swing length should be based on your own fitness and flexibility; the definitive top of backswing position may not be appropriate for you.

1 It is not absolutely necessary that you swing to the horizontal, but it is important that you try (pending flexibility) to turn the shoulders through 90 degrees. The combination of a shorter length of arc with a full shoulder turn is more effective than a full shoulder turn with a 'forced' backswing that reaches near horizontal.

2 The overswing is often linked to a poor turn during the backswing. A lateral hip movement with a shoulder tilt frequently creates a collapse of the left arm (below), and sometimes this error in the type of turn is

The pressure placed on the swing by trying to force a full length of arc will cause loss of control (left). It is more effective to make a full shoulder turn and shorten the length of the backswing.

influenced by a poor grip, or tension to the extent of delaying the 'set'.

3 A common sight is an excessive left heel lift which can give the hips too much freedom to turn. The right leg can lock again forcing the weight on to the left side,

An excessive heel lift provides the hips too much freedom to turn (above), causing the weight to fall on to the left side. The left arm collapses and the club overswings.

and this is termed a reverse pivot, which encourages the left arm to collapse.

4 The short swing is more often caused by poor technique as opposed to flexibility. Frequently golfers start the hands and arms independently of the turn; the swing unit outpaces the body, and resistance occurs at a certain stage which forces a premature downswing start.

If the hands and arms move independently of the body (right), a point of resistance will be reached which restricts the natural progression of the backswing.

5 At the start of the swing, try to 'feel' control over the extent you lift the left heel. Moreover, consider keeping it down completely. Continue and monitor the turn progressing around the swing axis and retaining the flex in the right leg – this will help to tighten the swing.

As the left side responds at the start of the swing (above), control the left heel lift and retain the flex in the right leg.

Practise simulating your backswing using a reference to build your turn around a central axis (above). It is best to do this facing a mirror or a window at home.

6 To provide freedom to lengthen your swing, a tension-free set up is important. Work on creating unity at the takeaway, allowing the left side to respond with the hands and arms. You should 'feel' that

The left hand 'smooths' the club away from the ball (above) and the left side responds in unison.

as the trunk turns, the arms swing in time.

Action of the legs and feet

The movement of the feet and legs during the swing is a combination of a reaction response and conscious movement, and here we will examine their role.

1 When you take your stance, the feet should be shoulder width apart with the left foot turned outwards slightly, and the right foot set at right angles to the target line. Flexing the knees correctly influences your balance and weight distribution and sets a foundation on which the swing can function.

2 During the takeaway the left hip will pull the knee

inwards towards the ball. This is not a conscious move but a reaction to the turn. The right knee during the backswing retains its flex; these positions are vital to the actions during the downswing.

As the swing starts, the hip turn pulls the left knee towards the ball (below). During the backswing the right knee retains its flexed position. The feet should be shoulder width apart for a full iron shot, the right foot set at right angles to the target line with the left foot slightly closed.

3 If the turn during the backswing has produced a resistance and 'wound' effect between the upper and lower body, a re-coil will automatically initiate the downswing. The lateral leg drive that accommodates this move can have an element of conscious influence, although it must be controlled.

4 As the left hip unwinds (below), it begins to pull the right foot counter-clockwise on to the toe, as the weight is fast transferring. The outside of the left foot acts as a resistance as the body unwinds. The throughswing will pull the right foot completely on to the toe.

The hands and arms have extended through impact (below right), completing the weight transfer. The body has unwound fully and pulled the right foot on to its toe.

The transition from backswing to downswing is like a rubber band wound around a propeller (above). As the full coil is reached at the top of the backswing, the legs and hips recoil – a reaction response, not a conscious movement.

Ball contact and arm swing

Poor ball striking is quite often the result of a general lack of confidence during the downswing. The player fails to retain the angle between left arm and club shaft, the wrists uncock early and sometimes the arms separate through impact.

1 Provided that you have started the swing well and 'timed' the wrist set on the backswing, the angle is retained on the downswing through a combination of lateral leg drive and leverage created by the left hand pulling. The 'timing' of the recovery (wrist uncock) is determined by the shot in hand. The left hand pulls the club head to descend and squeeze the ball between the

As the left side clears (above), the hands control the shaft recovery. Focus on 'squeezing' the ball between the club face and turf. At impact (above right), the club is realigned with the left arm.

club face and turf – the ball is already in flight and the leading edge of the club head cuts into the turf.

2 During this process, as the weight transfers the body unwinds, and the arms extend through impact along the target line. However, as the body continues to unwind, the club head moves back inside the line. As the body fully unwinds and begins to straighten, the arms fold naturally, and the hands finish at the side of the head.

The club head travels along the target line (right) until the arm swing pulls the club inside the line as the result of the unwinding left side.

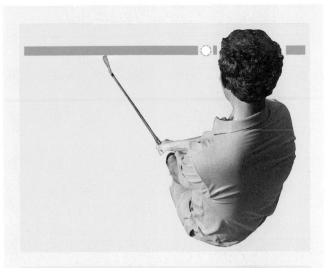

*The view from above (top)
shows how the body's pivotal
turn pulls the arm swing and
club head path back inside
the line as the follow through
progresses. The point at
which the arms begin to fold
into their finish position
(above). The shoulders turn
through 90 degrees. The finish
position (right).*

Insufficient power in long shots

Many golfers express a desire to increase distance yet all too often this is addressed by increasing swing speed. Countless times we see top professionals who are slight in stature hit the ball a significant distance, and this is achieved through sound technique and timing. The key is to identify the power leaks in your swing.

1 The path and plane of the swing will determine the angle of attack on the downswing which affects ball flight and distance. Furthermore, a good turn creating the 'feeling' of slight resistance between the upper and lower body is a major influence on these aspects.

To achieve a strong turn, check your posture at address (above). This helps promote a full swing arc also (below).

2 A poor start, swaying weight on to the right side through a lateral hip slide and left shoulder tilt, often positions so much weight on the right leg at the top of the swing that a 'spin out' and subsequent loss of power results in the downswing. A reverse pivot similarly shifts weight on to the right side as the downswing is in progress.

Poor posture can lead to swaying off the ball (left). The right leg straightens (below left) allowing excessive hip turn and placing too much weight on the left side at the top. The weight shift from a reverse pivot (below) forces the weight into the right side on the downswing and a consequent loss of power.

3 Tension at address leading to a takeaway that subdues the process of wrist set can encourage a left arm collapse, and the resulting 'cast' to regain downswing width is a major power leak.

The length and width of the swing arc provide power (right). As the left arm collapses, the width of arc is lost. The hands 'cast' the club to regain width, forcing the weight into the right side (below).

Full width of arc

Practice drill

1 Stand in front of a mirror or your reflection in a window. Go through your set up routine, waggle the club and build in subtle movement to keep you loose prior to the start. Concentrate on turning around your swing centre to maintain balance and to ensure that the power is stored in the turn.

2 Feel the downswing speed increase gradually, retaining the angle in order to time the recovery (not prematurely uncocking) so that the club accelerates through the impact area.

Develop a strong turn by using a reference point as an axis to turn around (above). Allow the wrist set to function to maintain a full width of arc. The slightly earlier recovery (left) has promoted a sweeping action and a shallow angle of attack similar to that of a driver.

Difficulty playing long irons

During the early stages of progression, new entrants to golf begin to practise with the long irons and frequently find that in addition to general inconsistency they strike the medium irons a greater distance. Consequently, the long irons are then isolated in the bag and rarely used.

The realization of difficulty is often increased as the player looks down from address and 'feels' a longer club with less face loft. This induces the player to swing fast, mistiming the correct sequence of movements in the golf swing, and attempting to manipulate the ball into the air.

At impact with a short iron (below) the shaft is more upright than with a long iron. To achieve a steeper angle of attack, position the ball centre or rear of centre (above), and the angle is *retained longer between the left arm and club shaft. At impact with a long iron (below) the shaft is flatter and the wrists uncock earlier, promoting a shallow angle of attack.*

FAULT FINDERS

1 When using the 8 and 9 irons, pitching wedge and sand wedge, we progressively need a higher flight. The concept of ball strike requires a descending angle of attack in order to produce height. The further the ball is moved to the rear of the stance, the steeper the angle of attack and subsequent initial height, and you will feel how the angle is retained longer during the downswing.

2 Conversely, with a long iron you stand further from the ball, and the lie of the club is flatter than for the sand wedge inducing a flatter swing plane. In keeping with the lower progressive trajectory required from a long iron, the ball is positioned further forward in the stance, inducing a slightly earlier recovery and a more shallow angle of attack, sweeping the ball away. Swing smoothly and trust your swing.

Difficulty playing fairway woods

The lie of the ball and level of terrain are primary factors when considering a long iron or fairway wood shot. The margin for error is clearly smaller than when playing a short iron, and therefore at an early stage of learning, confine yourself to playing these shots when the ball lies well and the ground is level.

1 At address the ball is positioned one ball inside the left heel (below). Later, when you do play from less favourable conditions, a bare lie will require the ball to be positioned slightly further back in your stance with a subtle amount of weight positioned into the left side. This induces the slightly steeper angle of attack necessary from this position.

2 Many golfers attempt to consciously lift the ball into the air, trying to nip it from the grass (below).

3 Similar to the long iron, the longer shaft and flatter lie promote a flatter swing plane (compared to a short iron) and this induces a slightly earlier recovery of the angle. The descent of the club head is at a shallower angle and, in a similar way to the driver, the bottom of the arc passes momentarily horizontally as the ball is swept away.

4 At address the left arm and club shaft form a straight line. It is important that you do not push the hands forward, as this decreases the club face loft and affects recovery of the angle during the downswing.

Note: When playing long irons and fairway woods it is important to remain relaxed at address and allow an uninhibited swing to respond, rather than contriving to gain height and distance.

As the weight transfers (top), the hands influence an earlier recovery. As the left arm and club shaft realign (left), the club head momentarily passes horizontal to the ground just before sweeping the ball away.

Taking a divot
with the driver

The driver contains the least amount of loft on the club face, and it therefore requires a sound swing accurately timing the delivery of club head to ball. A good understanding of the sequence of swing moves can utilize the advantage of teeing the ball as opposed to playing fairway woods and long irons.

1 Golfers frequently position the ball to the rear of the stance which will not provide the swing unit the time or room to recover the angle between the left arm and club shaft (below). The steep descent may produce a divot or a skyed shot.

2 A reverse pivot where the hips turn to excess will position weight on the left side during the backswing (below). This instinctively shifts to the right on the downswing, again trapping the club steeply in to the ball. Similarly, a poor start that pulls the shoulder down to tilt, will encourage the right side to come over the top or spin. Again, the angle of attack is too steep for the driver.

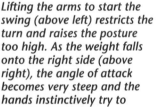

Lifting the arms to start the swing (above left) restricts the turn and raises the posture too high. As the weight falls onto the right side (above right), the angle of attack becomes very steep and the hands instinctively try to

manipulate the ball into the air. As the weight shifts to the right side at the start of the downswing (below), the right side comes over the top of the ball causing an out-to-in swing path.

3 At address the stance is slightly wider than shoulder width, the ball is positioned opposite the left heel with the shaft and left arm forming a straight line. Refer to pages 9-11 to review the pre-shot routine that ensures the correct driver/ball position.

If you have 'timed' the wrist set correctly on the backswing you are in a good position to execute the downswing.

A flatter lie at address with a driver (right) promotes a shallow swing plane during the downswing. The hands control an earlier recovery (below).

4 The longer shaft and flatter swing plane induces a *slightly* earlier recovery, allowing the club head to pass the bottom of the arc and sweep the ball off the tee (right).

As the club head approaches the bottom of its arc (right), it travels horizontal to the ground just before impact. As the ball is swept from the tee (below), the club head begins to travel on an upward plane.

CHAPTER THREE

Chipping and pitching

Thinned chip shots

The concept of ball striking and the sequence of ball-turf are vital factors in successful short game play. A common fault is a reluctance to impose club head descent on the ball, frequently resulting in thinned chip shots.

1 Initially stand with your feet approximately 12 inches apart (left), establishing square alignment with the ball just inside the left foot. Withdraw the left foot (bottom left) two or

With the feet angled (below), the weight will move into the left side when the knees flex 70:30. Lower your posture to accommodate the shorter club and press your hands in front of the club head.

three inches and turn it slightly outwards – this pulls the weight sufficiently into the left side when you flex your knees.

> **Note:** The shoulders remain parallel with the target line.

2 Flex the knees to accommodate gripping the club lower to afford you more control. The hands should lead the club head at address.

3 A clear understanding of the difference in swing action for chipping versus that for pitching is frequently lacking in many golfers. Study the two and you will see how they are frequently used in the wrong situation.

The length of swing and type of wrist set *often* used to *chip* are actually appropriate to the soft pitch shot, and this confusion restricts short game progress.

As the hands start the club away (above), the wrists set inwards to hood the club face.

This inward set is shown more clearly (top) with the hooded club face. The re-set realigns the left arm and club shaft at impact (above).

4 There are two ways to play the chip and run shot. The initial motion of the swing unit includes what is called an 'inward set' of the wrist – a very subtle move that retains the back of the left hand and club face facing the hole (unlike the pitch shot).

Allow a responsive, not conscious, move from the legs to accommodate the back- and through swings. The re-setting of the wrists

The re-set is held through the impact position (above). Focus on the club face and the back of the left hand moving towards the target.

pulls the club head to either nip or squeeze the ball depending on the lie. The through swing extends just beyond the left side. The alternative is simply to retain the swing unit during motion with no set.

Judging pace on chip and run shots

Survey the ground between the ball and the hole. Depending on the length of shot, and the level and speed of the green, visualize the height of ball flight and a landing point that would allow the ball to run to the hole.

1 Poor shot management

frequently results in leaving the ball short or running it past the hole. An uphill chip

When chipping uphill (below), a lofted club producing a high soft flight may lack sufficient momentum for the ball to run up to the hole.

played with a lofted club may not provide sufficient forward momentum to land the ball and propel it forwards to the hole. Conversely, a downhill chip on a fast green played with a straight-faced club will be too 'hot' to control. The

A firm chip with a straight-faced club to an uphill pin position lands with sufficient momentum to run to the hole.

club selection in the foregoing examples should be reversed.

2 After you have selected the club and the landing point, it is important that you remain 'focused' on that point. If you look towards the hole,

Remember that the hole is a secondary element; if you land the ball in the correct place, it then becomes the primary element.

your senses cannot get tuned to pitch the ball where you have chosen, and frequently you will overrun the hole.

3 Remember to allow for contours because once the ball has landed it will react like a putt and break accordingly; on severe upslopes, leave your chip short of the hole for the favourable putt.

When the ball lands and rolls from a chip shot it is affected by green contours as in putting. Read the break and select your landing point accordingly.

4 In general, select the chip and run over the pitch when you are on fairly level terrain around the perimeter of the green, and you do not have a hazard between you and the hole. The chip and run is often thought of as a safe shot because when it lands (usually on the green) the bounce and roll are fairly predictable. However, an exception, where you might select the pitch versus the

The ball is cushioned by the grass and stops too quickly (above). In this situation use a lofted club to land the ball on the putting surface.

chip and run, is when the pin is at the front of the green and you are short, requiring you to bounce and run the ball over the fairway. The uncertain reaction of the ball in this situation may be more suited to the soft pitch.

5 Because the club face position during this short swing is retained to face the target, it is important that the length of shot does not require the hands to reach hip height where the club would be horizontal. If you persist, and try and play chip and run shots from this position, too much pressure is placed on the hands and wrists; the length of swing requires a wrist set action appropriate to the pitch shot.

The length of swing places too much pressure on the hands and wrists when using the wrist set action for the chip and run. The technique (right) should be

interchanged with the pitch action (below).

Judging pitching distance

Unlike driving and iron play, you will be faced with certain shots that you have not had to play for some time around the green. Therefore, the practice swing is a primary factor in judging distance. For all shots, it will simulate 'feel' for the length of swing and strength of the stroke required.

Learn the versatility of your pitching clubs – most manufacturers vary face loft and sole design, which will affect distance, height and playability from certain lies.

For the short chip (below) the club has been taken back too far. A decelerating downswing (inset) causes the left elbow to buckle.

● With rare exceptions, virtually every shot we play in golf requires the swing speed to accelerate through the impact area. There is a correlation between swing speed and backswing length for chipping and pitching. Based on the principle of acceleration through impact, the player who swings the club back too far cannot accelerate downswing speed for fear of over-hitting. Therefore, he instinctively decelerates downswing speed to reach the target. The following exercise will enable you to understand the versatility and optimum backswing length for various distances.

Practice drill

1 On the practice ground, place targets at 10-foot intervals from 30 feet to 80 feet.

2 Begin by establishing a comfortable backswing length, allowing for controlled acceleration to the 30-foot target. Continue by aiming at the 40-foot target, and increase the downswing acceleration while retaining the same backswing length as used for 30 feet.

3 Based on the principle of acceleration through impact, this drill will teach you how much you can increase distance while retaining the same backswing length. The exercise enhances your perception of the versatility of swing length as it relates to distance.

Establish the length of backswing for a 25-foot pitch using practice swings (below left). For a 35-foot pitch (below), using the same backswing length, accelerate firmer on the downswing.

Difficulty with the pitch shot

Golfers tend to find pitching more difficult than the chip and run, particularly the 'soft and subtle' pitch frequently needed around the green. There is little room for any compromise in the descending downswing and subsequent ball/turf contact that is so vital when pitching with the short irons.

The set up for the pitch is essentially the same as for the chip and run, although the emphasis changes depending on the numerous lies to be encountered around the green itself.

1 In general, the stance is

slightly wider with a greater proportion of weight on the left side to assist the delivery of the club (opposite left).

2 As the swing starts, the wrists begin to 'set' as the hands pass the right knee (opposite right). The club face position has been influenced by the greater extent of turn for the pitch versus chip and run. The arms swing upwards (according to the length of shot) and a responsive versus conscious amount of turn accommodates the hands and arms to conclude the backswing.

3 A firm leverage is created by the left hand pulling, initiating the downswing simultaneously with response from the legs that must assist –not resist.

The set is a gradual process that blends within the swing motion (above). Unlike the wrist set for the chip the club face and back of the left hand positions have altered in

response to the turn (top right). The left hand leads to retain the descending angle on the ball (above).

4 At the point of impact and extension, the back of the left hand and club face resist to retain their position facing the hole.

Note: The club head significantly accelerates down and through the impact area to withstand the solid ball/turf contact.

The legs respond by moving laterally at the target as the hands lead the club head just prior to impact (above). The position of the club face and back of the left hand are held through impact (left) and retained into the follow through.

The follow through

The follow through on the chip and run (right) is shorter with the club head staying low to the ground. The follow through (below) is progressing into a higher finish.

Overcoming errors in alignment

1 The principle of correct target alignment requires the club head at address to be positioned on the target line (below) with an imaginary line across the player's feet, knees, hips and shoulders set parallel with the target line.

2 The common misconception is an attempt to align the body with the target line (right). This is incorrect and furthermore the attempt to

achieve this position usually makes the problem worse.

Alignment set up drill

Understanding the theory in principle is one thing; the only way this can then be utilized consistently during the address position is via the use of a systematic approach to the set up.

Ground the club and step forward with the right foot (below left). Visualize a line from the ball to a reference point and set a line across the right toe, knees, hips and shoulders parallel with the target line, then position the left foot. To check alignment (below) lay a club across your toes, and a second club (bottom) extending from the ball parallel with the first club. The second club should aim at the target.

Bunker play

Poor bunker shots

A common problem exists in the way many golfers set up for pitch/chip shots and for greenside bunker shots.

1 The square set up (below left) will not promote the descending angle of attack required for both types of shots; this is because the left hip blocks the passage of the hands and arms influencing an early recovery. Furthermore, for the sand shot in particular, this set up will not allow the swing path necessary for the shot to function effectively.

2 Conversely, many golfers understand the concept of set up and swingpath yet exaggerate certain points that restrict potential. It is

common to see a player set up too open in the stance (below right), and open the club face to excess. The outside/inside swing path is so acute that the ball will not travel any distance.

3 Either lack of confidence, or a misconceived approach results in the player trying to 'nip' the ball off the top of the sand. Conversely, another common fault is an immediate wrist set and a 'quitted' follow through. The next section examines the ball/strike concept for sand shots.

CHAPTER FOUR

Technique for greenside sand shots

In order that you can develop eventually a playing routine for this shot, first establish your set up through the following drill.

Note: It is because many golfers exaggerate the open stance that I want you to establish the square position first – then open.

Practice drill

1 Take your address position with two clubs on the ground to establish normal square alignment; the ball at this stage is just inside the left heel. Hold the club between the thumb and forefinger of your right hand and lay the club slightly 'open' (in relation to the target line (right)); and assemble the grip fully.

2 Now withdraw the left foot (below) and turn the right foot inwards slightly. The knee flex (below right) will now automatically place the weight into the left side (70 per cent); the ball position is now more central. The feet, knees, hips and shoulders are now all open – to a controlled extent.

Ball/strike concept

1 When taking your stance in sand, 'dig' the feet under the surface, to secure your foundation and also give you a 'feel' for the texture and depth of the sand.

2 Recall for a moment the concept of striking an iron shot. It is quite the opposite with the sand shot. The open face utilizes the design concept of the club's sole

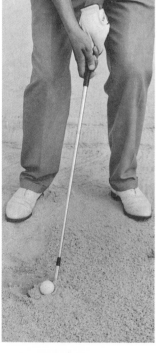

during the downswing the club slides underneath the ball (above). With the iron shot we emphasised the concept of 'squeezing' the ball between the face and the turf; but at the moment of impact with the sand shot, the ball flies out on a pocket

of sand. In fact, in many cases the club face never makes contact with the ball (above). Because conditions vary so much, rather than adopting a fixed thought of hitting one or two inches behind the ball, practise the 'feel' of sliding the club under the ball. The club head in effect is 'stunning' the sand below the ball. The cushion of sand between the ball and club face quickly makes you realize how firmly these shots should be struck.

The pocket of sand subdues the speed of the swing at impact (top) and therefore firm acceleration is required. The club face slides under the ball (right) but you should focus on striking the tee, not the ball. Practise the feel of *sliding the club under the ball by playing shots off a tee (above).*

3 The wrists set early but not immediately; the swing unit starts in motion, as the hands pass the right knee the wrists begin to set. Although a steep angle is formed, the wrist set 'blends' with the motion. The body turn, although not full, responds to allow freedom of movement, and the weight remains on the left side. The open nature of the set up influences the backswing path to move outside the target line (above).

The wrists begin to break (above right) as the hands pass the right knee at takeaway. This action blends into the swing motion. To start the downswing (right) the left hand leads firmly and the legs drive laterally.

4 A lateral leg drive in unison with a firm left hand pull initiates the downswing. As the club slides under the ball (above), the acceleration pulls the hands and arms wide through the shot, with the back of the left hand and club face retaining their position (right).

Sand texture and strike drill

Generally speaking, the downswing requires firm acceleration on most greenside trap shots including those from varying sand texture. There are, of course, exceptions although we will deal with the norm. The grade of sand found in the majority of bunkers on British inland courses is generally coarse and heavier than that used in certain new golf developments or at seaside links. The light soft texture of the latter can require a more authoritative stroke, particularly if the sand has been thinned extensively and fluffed up through raking. Wet sand of any kind requires a committed downswing to withstand the compacted sand condition.

Practice drill

You should practise this exercise to increase 'feel' for the concept of striking greenside sand shots.

Tee the ball up in the bunker; as you set up, visualize the tee and feel that you are going to slide the club under the ball and take the tee from under it. If you do this exercise correctly the ball will pop up; it may or may not leave the trap but it will provide the feel appropriate to the shot.

Fairway trap shots

When a tee shot lands in a fairway trap there are a number of considerations to take before playing the shot.

If you consider that the green is reachable, what are the risks involved and the likelihood of success regarding the green's defences? Is it well trapped? Are there ditches, water hazards, or further bunkers short of the green that a slight mishit will find? Is it a par 5 where maximum distance is not crucial?

If confident of a long recovery, have you taken into account further hazards and a level lie for the next shot?

1 Stand to the side of the trap and consider how far back you are from the lip and its height; visualize the flight of your initial club selection (opposite top) and realistically determine the feasibility of your first instinct. If the trap is built with a slight upslope this is to your advantage; conversely, a slight

downslope will make a long recovery more difficult. Even if you are sufficiently to the rear of the trap and the ball

If the ball lies on a downslope (above) or a poor lie, recovery with a straight-faced club is always difficult.

appears to lie well, is it in a
slight trough?

2 As you near making a
decision regarding strategy,
clarify during your visualization whether you intend to
strike the ball totally clean or
with a semi-sand contact.

*When initial height is
important (above), play the
shot with a semi-sand
contact. Determine your
strategy for the type of 'strike'
(right) before setting up.*

3 Slide your feet into the sand, the full swing requires stability. There is a small margin for error at the point of contact which places a higher premium on control and timing the sequence of swing movements.

Putting

Judging distance
for long putts

As you look towards the hole, when you are preparing to putt, the realization of distance filters through to your senses and you adjust the strength and length of stroke accordingly.

This acknowledgement of distance is helpful, although at best it is a guess on our part. Being able to judge distance accurately gives the golfer greater reliability and success in putting.

Practice drill

1 On the green, measure a three-foot putt using a rule for accuracy.

2 Stand over your ball, and look down visualizing a line from the ball extending 12 inches, and stop.

3 Proceed and visually extend the line another 12 inches to two feet, and stop. Continue to visualize the final 12 inches to the hole.

4 For a putt of approximately 10 feet, identify the first three feet accurately in this way. Because you instinctively know what constitutes three feet you can visualize a complete increment of three feet and stop, then continue visualizing the next increment of three feet, and then the final 12 inches to the hole (10 feet in total).

5 For a 10-foot putt therefore, you establish the first three-foot increments of 12 inches, and then complete increments of three feet.

6 For excessively long putts you establish the first 10 feet using the foregoing method and then continue visualizing complete increments of 10 feet to the hole; the balance of distance left over for odd lengths is easily judged.

7 You can now take this concept on to the putting green and it can be used as a 'yardstick'. Measure various distances using the foregoing method and, as you make practice swings, retain in your memory the specific distance you have judged. When you strike the putts you can now begin to correlate length and weight of stroke with the accurate judgement of distance merging the two for greater consistency.

CHAPTER FIVE

Loss of putting confidence

I once read a newspaper report based on the loss of confidence experienced by a highly placed professional in the world rankings. The player had been working to correct a technical fault in his stroke that had greatly affected his putting over the previous two months. It had reached the stage where he felt tension and anxiety because he was scared of missing putts. This feeling happens to all golfers and yet if we let it go on, unchallenged, it takes the initiative and subdues any chance of improvement – instead, it rules us.

The fact is that if you are *scared* of missing putts you cannot get the confidence to hole putts. The mental over-effort used to correct the stroke and avoid missing, attracts the very outcome you are trying to avoid – it encourages negative tension. However, this does not mean that you should approach putting casually, not caring whether you hole or miss putts.

I strongly suggest that if you are to release and allow your instinctive ability to function, that you retain a rationale and never be scared of missing a putt or any shot. None of us should be so complacent that we expect and sometimes demand that we hole every putt, but, again, do not interpret this as negative thinking.

As you stand over a putt, retain the inner desire, the confidence and courage to hole it, yet control these emotions. At the same time be rational, and accept that you may miss but don't be scared of doing so. When you sense that these irrational thoughts are taking over, stop. Think for a moment and challenge them. Can't you see that they are dictating the terms of how you should feel and act?

Spontaneous putting

If you feel so inclined, allow the aggression of this realization to release you from the hold it had, and then putt uninhibitedly. Where over-concern had forced you previously to become too preoccupied with your problems, the sudden freedom will often rekindle an improved stroke spontaneously.

This will assist your thought process greatly. Furthermore, it will often self-correct a technical problem. However, if further work is required to

repair the technique, it now becomes easier because you have reconciled the major problem.

You may well have fallen into a common trap: you may have worked on the stroke and improved technique, yet retained the same thought process. This vicious circle can undermine the stroke you have worked to improve.

When you experience the ball rolling past the hole on a missed putt (which we all have to face), refuse to allow this to influence a negative flow of adrenaline or a hot or cold sweat (common symptoms with loss of confidence). Instead, treat a miss with mere contempt, and learn to control your own emotions.

Lining up putts

Learning visualization is the key to lining up putts accurately. When you see players crouching behind the ball, focusing on the line, what are they visualizing? The practice putting green is the place to learn the process, develop it and then use it on the course.

1 Begin with straight putts: from 6 feet, crouch a sufficient distance behind the ball that allows you to focus your eyeline as low as possible (approximately 10

feet behind the ball).

Practise total concentration for 30 seconds; focus your eyeline on the ball position, and slowly progress your eyeline forwards drawing a line in your mind's eye directly to the hole. If you do this slowly you will sense a change in contour as your focus graduates forwards. Firstly start with short distances, as you increase distance – visualize the line for 30 seconds to begin with – then putt 6 balls.

2 When you face a break putt, establish first the extent of break the ball would take on a straight line to the hole. This realization, and the image it provides will now enable you to begin reading break. Your 'feel' for the degree of break if you putted at the hole will enhance your senses to now begin visualizing the curvature of roll to account for break.

The lower you position your eyeline (above) the more clearly you can read the line. From the ball, focus your eyeline along the grass, trying to imagine the ball rolling at the hole.

When reading break, visualize the ball rolling at the hole (above) to determine at what point it would break. Then try to visualize your allowance for break.

Time management

Use your time effectively on the greens if you are first to putt. Players in your group and in the match behind might be waiting for you to play, and this sometimes causes golfers to rush. In this situation, make sure you are first to the green, moving promptly so that the necessary time is available to gain the composure and concentration to read line.

Conversely, if you are last to putt in a group of 3 or 4, you can use your time even more effectively, reading line from different angles while your playing partners are putting.

Aiming the putter

Accurately aiming the putter during the set up is crucial in order to utilize the potential gained from the line and pace techniques previously outlined.

Practice drill

Practise the following routine on the practice putting green, commencing with a 3-foot straight putt, and then gradually increasing the length.

1 Place your putter next to the hole and you will notice that the distance between the toe and heel is approximately the same as the width of the hole (opposite). Therefore when you place the putter behind the ball for a straight 3-foot putt you are setting the putter into 'track' (the two parallel lines that extend from the heel and toe of the putter, directly to each edge of the hole). Assuming a 'true' putting surface, if your stroke was 'slotted in' and passing through this track as you struck the ball, you would hole the putt every time.

2 The key therefore on a putt you have deemed straight is to visualize the 'track' and set the putter into it. A common fault, which I am sure you have observed watching other golfers, is the constant regripping and 'positioning' of the putter face. Once the 'track' is seen, the putter should be systematically set into position and this should not be altered.

PUTTING

3 Make the usual practice strokes to simulate 'feel' (opposite), then take a short step forwards with your right foot positioned slightly behind the line of the ball. Note that the left foot is trailing the right.

4 Carefully slide the putter 'into track' (far left), slowly turn the head and focus along the track to verify that you are tracked correctly. Place the left

foot just wide of the ball and slide the right into position (far right).

5 On a break putt, visualize the initial line the ball has to take and set the putter into its track accordingly (below).

6 On all putts, particularly short putts under 10 feet, use the routine on page 96 to keep your stroke on track.

Putting routine

Do not watch the ball roll towards the hole anticipating whether or not you have holed the putt. The premature movement of the upper body and head not only takes the putter 'out of track', but it affects the acceleration of the stroke in progress also. Wait for the sound of the ball to hit the back of the hole. Use this key and you won't compromise the line and speed of your stroke. Obviously you will miss putts yet the rule of 'waiting for the sound' will increase the amount of putts you hole.